CELEBRATING THE FAMILY NAME OF SINGH

Celebrating the Family Name of Singh

Walter the Educator

Silent King Books
a WhichHead Entertainment Imprint

Copyright © 2024 by Walter the Educator

All rights reserved. No part of this book may be reproduced in any manner whatsoever without written permission except in the case of brief quotations embodied in critical articles and reviews.

First Printing, 2024

Disclaimer

This book is a literary work; the story is not about specific persons, locations, situations, and/or circumstances unless mentioned in a historical context. Any resemblance to real persons, locations, situations, and/or circumstances is coincidental. This book is for entertainment and informational purposes only. The author and publisher offer this information without warranties expressed or implied. No matter the grounds, neither the author nor the publisher will be accountable for any losses, injuries, or other damages caused by the reader's use of this book. The use of this book acknowledges an understanding and acceptance of this disclaimer.

Celebrating the Family Name of Singh is a memory book that belongs to the Celebrating Family Name Book Series by Walter the Educator. Collect them all and more books at WaltertheEducator.com

USE THE EXTRA SPACE TO DOCUMENT YOUR FAMILY MEMORIES THROUGHOUT THE YEARS

SINGH

Beneath the sun, where courage reigns,

The name of Singh forever remains.

A lion's heart, a spirit free,

A name that echoes through history.

Born of valor, fierce and true,

The Singhs are strength in all they do.

With every step, they pave the way,

A legacy bold as the break of day.

In fields of gold and battles vast,

The Singh name stands, a force steadfast.

Through trials faced with fearless might,

They rise, unyielding, to the fight.

From sacred words in hallowed halls,

To roaring chants where duty calls,

The Singh name thrives, a guiding star,

A flame that shines both near and far.

With turbans high and heads held tall,

The Singhs bring justice to us all.

Their wisdom flows like rivers wide,

Their honor gleams with boundless pride.

Through songs of faith and swords of steel,

The name of Singh inspires and heals.

A family strong, a voice so clear,

Their presence cherished far and near.

With hearts of gold and roots so deep,

The Singhs their sacred promises keep.

Through every dawn and every night,

Their path is lit by inner light.

The lion roars within their soul,

A symbol bold, a noble goal.

Through unity, their strength is shown,

A family proud, a league of their own.

From ancient lands to modern day,

The Singh name charts a steadfast way.

A lineage vast, a truth profound,

In every heart, their echoes sound.

So sing of Singh, both fierce and kind,

A name of courage, heart, and mind.

Forever honored, strong, and free,

The Singhs remain in history's tree.

ABOUT THE CREATOR

Walter the Educator is one of the pseudonyms for Walter Anderson. Formally educated in Chemistry, Business, and Education, he is an educator, an author, a diverse entrepreneur, and he is the son of a disabled war veteran. "Walter the Educator" shares his time between educating and creating. He holds interests and owns several creative projects that entertain, enlighten, enhance, and educate, hoping to inspire and motivate you. Follow, find new works, and stay up to date with Walter the Educator™ at WaltertheEducator.com

www.ingramcontent.com/pod-product-compliance
Lightning Source LLC
LaVergne TN
LVHW012052070526
838201LV00082B/3922